Teens and Sex

Other titles in the *Teen Choices* series include:

Teens and Bullying

Teens and Drinking

Teens and Marijuana

Teens and Sexting

Teens and Smoking

TEEN
Choices

Teens and Sex

Andrea C. Nakaya

ReferencePoint
Press®

San Diego, CA

For more information, contact:
ReferencePoint Press, Inc.
PO Box 27779
San Diego, CA 92198
www.ReferencePointPress.com

LIBRARY OF CONGRESS CATALOGING-IN-PUBLICATION DATA

Nakaya, Andrea C., 1976-
  Teens and sex / by Andrea C. Nakaya.
     pages cm. -- (Teen choices)
  Includes bibliographical references and index.
   ISBN-13: 978-1-60152-912-1 (hardback)
   ISBN-10: 1-60152-912-0 (hardback)
  1. Teenagers--Sexual behavior--United States--Juvenile literature. 2. Sexual ethics--United States--Juvenile literature. 3. Sexual ethics for teenagers--United States--Juvenile literature. I. Title.
   HQ27.N35 2016
   306.708350973--dc23

                                                                    2015017842

Contents

A Life-Changing Choice

Garrison is a seventeen-year-old high school student. He says that the topic of sex is inescapable for him and his friends: "I feel that sex is a vital part of the social culture at school." It is a frequent topic of conversation. Sex plays an important part in reputations and social status, with students being judged on what they have—or have not—done sexually, often based on rumors about their behavior. Overall, he says, "Sex plays a huge social dynamic in our teenage years."[1] Other teens echo Garrison's statement that sex plays a significant role in their lives. For example, sixteen-year-old Elizabeth says that at her school, "you can't go an hour without hearing the word, or some other reference to it."[2] Every day teens like Garrison and Elizabeth are faced with the topic of sex, and they must make choices about how to act sexually. Research shows that a little less than half will choose to have sex, and a little more than half will choose not to.

A Big Deal

These choices are important because sex is a big deal, with numerous potential consequences. First, it can completely change the way people feel about themselves and others. Some teens say that having sex is a good experience because it is pleasurable and it helps them feel a strong connection with someone they care about. However, others report that because sex involves such intense emotions, it can make relationships more complicated and breakups more difficult. Sex can also transform a person's reputation. Sometimes this transformation is for the better, and sometimes it is for the worse; overall, though, many teens report that their friends treat them quite differently after they find out that they have had sex.

Finally, in addition to impacting emotions and reputations, sex can result in life-changing and sometimes life-threatening risks. One of these is the risk of sexually transmitted diseases (STDs). Statistics show that STDs are quite common among US teens. In 2015 the Centers for Disease Control and Prevention (CDC) released its most recent data showing that in 2013 almost ten thousand US youths were diagnosed with HIV, the sexually transmitted virus that causes AIDS. Both HIV and AIDS are incurable, necessitating a lifetime of medication (often with unpleasant side effects). And although medications to control both have greatly improved in recent years, people still die of AIDS.

Another life-altering risk is pregnancy. In 2015 the National Campaign to Prevent Teen and Unplanned Pregnancy reported that more than 270,000 teenage girls had babies in 2013. The overall teen pregnancy rate was even higher because many teen pregnancies end in miscarriage or abortion instead of birth. In fact, the US Department of Health and Human Services estimates that only about 60 percent of teen pregnancies actually end in a live birth. Data show that US teen pregnancy and birth rates have been improving since the 1950s, but both remain relatively high compared to the rest of the developed world.

> "Sex plays a huge social dynamic in our teenage years."[1]
>
> —Garrison, a high school student.

On the website of a global HIV/AIDS organization based in the United Kingdom, a girl who calls herself "Laura 2" explains how having sex without knowing the potential consequences completely changed her life. She explains, "I have never had sex ed. but my boyfriend had had it, he explained it to me and answered any questions—I said I wanted to try it and he asked if I was on the pill and I said yes, but I didn't have a clue about what he was talking about. We had sex." She says, "A month later and my period had been 3 weeks late so I went to my

One unintended—and life-changing—consequence of teen sex is pregnancy. According to statistics, more than a quarter of a million teens gave birth in the United States in 2013.

GP [general practitioner] and he confirmed I was pregnant. I asked how it had happened and he gave me the science part of sex ed."[3] She now has an eleven-month-old daughter. She insists that young people need to be educated about their sexual choices and their possible consequences before they have sex, not afterward as happened to her.

Being Informed and Thinking Ahead

Because engaging in sex can have life-altering consequences, it is important for teens to be informed and also to think about their values and choices. This can help avoid sexual situations in which a teen loses control and then regrets it later, such as having sex because of peer pressure, drug or alcohol use, or because it feels good in the moment.

Teens who think ahead about the possible consequences of sex, and about their own values, are more likely to make choices that make sense for them. For some teens, this might mean choosing to have sex. For example, Erin says that she and her boyfriend made the decision to have sex when she was seventeen years old. She explains, "After careful deliberation, we decided that we were both ready to have sex. I went on birth control and after waiting a couple of months to ensure its efficacy, we waited for the right time."[4] Erin says that as a result of making sure that sex was something they both understood and wanted, it ended up being a very fulfilling experience. For other teens though, thinking about the consequences and their own feelings regarding sex leads to the decision to wait. Stephanie says that she first had sexual intercourse at age sixteen, but for the rest of high school and college she resisted pressure to have sex with a lot of people like her friends were doing. She knew that this was not something that would make her happy. She says, "What's the point in getting naked with someone and putting myself in the most vulnerable position possible if I don't connect with him? They don't know me; I don't know them. Having sex like that seems like a nightmare."[5]

> "Some of the choices you make now could stay with you for the rest of your life."[6]
>
> —Sex educator Bronwen Pardes.

Whatever they decide, the choices teens make about becoming sexually active do matter. As sex education teacher Bronwen Pardes cautions, "Some of the choices you make now could stay with you for the rest of your life." For this reason, she warns, "it's important that they be well-informed and well thought out. Sex can be a wonderful, positive aspect of your life, and it can also lead to some serious consequences."[6]

Chapter One

About Teen Sex Today

A lot of teens are sexually active. That was true a decade ago, and it remains true today. In 2003, when the CDC surveyed high school students across the country, it found that 46.7 percent had engaged in sexual intercourse. The last time the CDC conducted that same survey, in 2013, the number was almost exactly the same: 46.8 percent said they had engaged in sexual intercourse. In other words, close to half of high school students report that they have had sex at least once, and that number has remained about the same for more than ten years. As these statistics show, sex is a topic that affects a large number of teens.

Teen Sex in the United States

The CDC is the most comprehensive source of information about the sexual behavior of US teens. Every two years since 1991 it has been conducting a national survey of high school students called the Youth Risk Behavior Survey. This survey monitors some of the main types of behavior that put youth at risk, including sexual behavior, and it provides details about numerous sexual activities and trends among teens. In addition to showing that almost half of all high school students have had sex, CDC statistics reveal that the number of females who have had sex compared to males is about the same. Although sexual activity does not vary much by gender, it does vary significantly by age: older teens are more likely to have had sex than younger teens. According to the CDC, about 64 percent of twelfth-graders have had sex, 54 percent of eleventh-graders, 41 percent of tenth-graders, and 30 percent of ninth-graders.

Only about 5 percent of students had sexual intercourse for the first time before they reached the age of thirteen.

While a large number of teens have had sex at least once, this does not necessarily mean teens are having a lot of sex. Research indicates that a much smaller percentage of teens are actually having sex on a regular basis or are having sex with a lot of people. The CDC found that although almost 47 percent of teens surveyed reported having sex before, only 39 percent were actually considered to be sexually active, meaning that they had had sex within three months of answering the survey. An even smaller percentage reported having had sex with lots of partners; only 15 percent said they had had sex with four or more people.

Demographic Differences

Studies show differences in teenage sexual behavior based on ethnicity. African American teens are more likely than white teens to have sex, to have multiple sex partners, and to engage in sex at a younger age. According to the CDC, about 44 percent of white high school students have had sex compared with about 61 percent of black students. Additionally, about 3 percent of white teens have had sex before the age of thirteen compared with 14 percent of black teens. Pregnancy rates are highest among African American teens, followed by Hispanic teens, and then white teens. The differences, experts say, are partly due to less frequent use of contraceptives by black and Hispanic teenagers.

Whereas the percentage of teens that have had sex is about the same for males and females, sexual behavior varies by gender. The CDC reports that males are more likely than females to engage in a number of behaviors that increase the risk of unintended pregnancy and STD infection. This includes having sex with multiple partners and using alcohol or drugs before engaging in sexual activity. In contrast, females are more likely to take steps to reduce the risks of pregnancy and STDs. These steps include contraceptive use and getting tested for HIV.

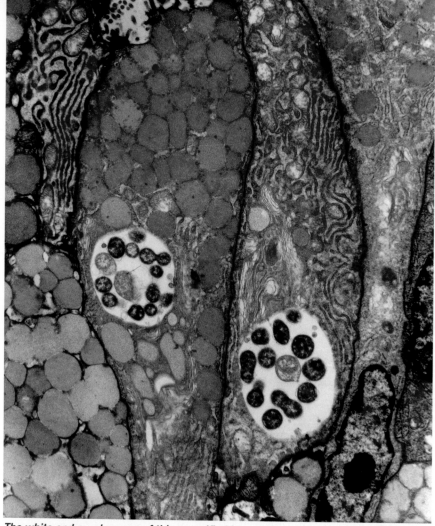

The white and purple areas of this magnified image show human cells infected with chlamydia. Chlamydia is the most common bacterial infection spread through sexual activity.

Research shows that the percentage of US teens who have sex is similar to what takes place in other developed nations. However, the United States has much higher rates of teen pregnancy and STDs than many other countries. In a 2014 report, the National Center for Health Statistics compares the United States to thirty other developed countries. It reports that teen birthrates in the United States are some of the highest. According to the report, the US teen birthrate is about twenty-six per one thousand teens. Only seven of the thirty countries analyzed had rates over twenty. In contrast, Japan, the Netherlands, and Switzerland all have rates at less than five in one thousand.

The Use of Contraception

Research shows that when teens do have sex, many use some type of protection against pregnancy and STDs, most commonly condoms or birth control pills. The CDC reports that about 60 percent of sexually active teens used a condom the last time they had sex, and almost 20 percent used birth control pills. A study published in *Women's Health Issues* in 2014 also shows that the majority of teens seem to be using contraception. In that study, researchers analyzed data about the sexual activity of thousands of people from 1982 to 2010. They found that the average age for young women in the United States to first have sex is about seventeen years old. Also, when compared to 1982, more are using contraceptives when they first have sex. Overall, they report that almost three-quarters of sexually active women say they used contraception the first time they had sex. However, the researchers also found that contraceptive use among Hispanic women lags significantly behind that of other ethnicities.

Even though many teens say they use some type of contraception, a lot of them do not use it every time they have sex or do not use it properly. Contraceptives work only when they are used—and used correctly. For instance, birth control pills need to be taken every day, and condoms must cover the entire penis and, to avoid possible tears, must not have any air bubbles. Dr. Rima Himelstein explains that when teens get excited, busy, or distracted, they sometimes forget about contraception or use it improperly. She says, "Condoms, birth control pills, the patch and the vaginal ring only work if they are used correctly. Between school, texting, sports, homework, texting, friends, Facebook, texting, music, eating, texting and sometimes sleeping, our teens R 2 BZ!"[7] Inconsistent or improper use of contraception puts teens at risk for STDs and pregnancy.

> "Between school, texting, sports, homework, texting, friends, Facebook, texting, music, eating, texting and sometimes sleeping, our teens R 2 BZ [to use contraception properly]!"[7]
>
> —Dr. Rima Himelstein.

Even as pregnancy rates for teens have gone down in recent years, partly because of increased use of contraception, the number of pregnant teens is not insignificant. The National Campaign to Prevent Teen and Unplanned Pregnancy says that nearly three in ten teens will become pregnant by age twenty. The majority of these pregnancies are unintentional. The Guttmacher Institute, which conducts research on teenage sexual trends, reports that of those teens who do become pregnant, about 60 percent give birth, 26 percent have abortions, and the rest miscarry.

Long-Acting Reversible Contraception

Because teens often fail to consistently use contraception, some doctors encourage the use of long-acting reversible contraception (LARC) methods. The two most common are intrauterine devices (IUD) and implants. An IUD is a small device that is inserted into the uterus; the contraceptive implant is a matchstick-sized rod that is inserted under the skin of the upper arm. Both methods require an office visit with a doctor. After insertion, both devices continuously work to prevent pregnancy: the IUD prevents fertilization of an egg, and the implant prevents ovulation. Protection typically lasts from three to ten years. In 2011 the American College of Obstetricians and Gynecologists stated that LARC methods are the most effective form of reversible contraception. Physician and college member Eve Espey explains that LARC methods are much less likely to fail than other types of birth control. She says, "The major advantage is that after insertion, LARCs work without having to do anything else. There's no maintenance required."[8]

Research shows that the use of LARC methods by teens has increased in recent years. For instance, the CDC analyzed the use of this type of contraception among young women aged fifteen to nineteen who sought contraception between 2005 and 2013 under the Title X National Family Planning Program. Title X provides family planning for low-income individuals. The study

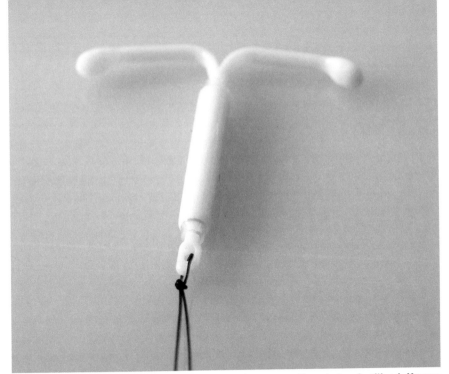

An IUD (pictured) prevents pregnancy by keeping an egg from being fertilized. Known as a long-acting reversible contraception (LARC) method, IUDs are becoming more popular among teens.

found that in 2013 about 7 percent of teens looking for contraception chose these long-acting types of contraception—most commonly implants—an increase from only 0.4 percent in 2005.

Oral Sex

Sexual intercourse is not the only sexual activity in which teens engage. Research shows that many teens have had oral sex—during which a person uses his or her mouth to stimulate the genitals of another person. In 2012 the CDC reported that about two-thirds of fifteen- to twenty-four-year-olds have had oral sex. The number who said they had oral sex before they had intercourse was about the same as those who said they had intercourse first.

In recent years reports have circulated about oral sex becoming increasingly common and casual among teens. Commenting on a *New York Times* article about sex, nineteen-year-old Johnny insists, "Oral sex is huge in this generation."[9] Some teens say that they have oral sex instead of intercourse because

Sexting

Many teens say that they have used their cell phones to send or receive sexually suggestive photographs or messages. This is called sexting. Some people warn that sexting can be harmful to teens because sexts can easily be viewed by people other than those intended, resulting in bullying or damage to a person's reputation. Counselor and author Raychelle Cassada Lohmann explains how: "Once a photo is out, there's no way of knowing how many people have saved it, tagged it, shared it, etc. Unfortunately the photo could re-surface years after it was taken and posted." In many states, sending a nude picture of a person under eighteen is considered child pornography and is thus illegal. Conviction for such an offense can result in jail time.

Despite the potential risks, sexting remains common. Some people point out that because teens communicate so much by cell phone, it is natural for some of that communication to be about sex. They see sexting as a type of flirting. In 2014 researchers from Drexel University in Pennsylvania surveyed 175 college students and found that many had sexted and that very few of them said they had suffered negative consequences. "We were struck by how many of those surveyed seem to think of sexting as a normal, standard way of interacting with their peers," says David DeMatteo, one of the study authors.

Raychelle Cassada Lohmann, "The Dangers of Teen Sexting," *Psychology Today*, July 20, 2012. www.psychology today.com.

Quoted in Randye Hoder, "Study Finds Most Teens Sext Before They're 18," *Time*, July 3, 2014. http://time.com.

it allows them to keep their virginity intact. Others have oral sex because they believe it is a good way to engage in sexual activity without risking pregnancy or an STD. For an article about teens and oral sex, writer Kori Ellis talked to several teens. One sixteen-year-old boy told her, "Girls want to remain virgins until they're married, but want to have some fun, too. I've run into quite a few who are willing to have oral or anal sex all the time, but still consider themselves virgins."[10] Although it is true that oral sex cannot result in pregnancy, in both males and females it can lead to a variety of STDs, including HIV, herpes, chlamydia, and gonorrhea.

Some teens say they have oral sex because they are trying to avoid intercourse. Evidence suggests that this strategy might not work. Some studies show that oral sex often leads to intercourse. In a study published in 2011 in the *Archives of Pediatrics and Adolescent Medicine*, for instance, researchers studied students from two public high schools in California. They found that oral sex seemed to lead to sexual intercourse. Most of the students who had oral sex reported that they had also ended up having sexual intercourse within six months of doing so. Overall, students who had oral sex during ninth grade were much more likely to have sexual intercourse by the end of eleventh grade than students who did not.

Despite evidence that oral sex does happen among teens and that it can lead to sexual intercourse, critics insist that worries about rampant casual oral sex among teens have been exaggerated. Researchers Joel Best and Kathleen A. Bogle researched teen sex behavior after hearing stories about promiscuous behavior among teens, such as teens giving oral sex to multiple people at sex parties. The researchers found that worries about all types of sexual behavior, including oral sex, had been inflated. They report, "There is little evidence that oral sex is rampant among the young."[11] They also did not find evidence that large numbers of teens are having oral sex instead of intercourse.

> "There is little evidence that oral sex is rampant among the young."[11]
>
> —Authors Joel Best and Kathleen A. Bogle.

Hookup Culture

Concerns have also surfaced in recent years that sex in general has become something that many teens view very casually. The concern is that sexually active teens are partnering with people they barely know rather than limiting sex to committed relationships. In a 2012 article in the *Review of General*

Psychology, researchers describe this trend, often referred to as *hookup culture*. They state,

> Hooking up—brief uncommitted sexual encounters among individuals who are not romantic partners or dating each other—has taken root within the sociocultural milieu of adolescents, emerging adults, and men and women throughout the Western world. Over the past 60 years, the prioritization of traditional forms of courting and pursuing romantic relationships has shifted to more casual "hookups."[12]

Donna Freitas is a college teacher. In 2006 she surveyed more than twenty-five hundred college students across the United States, and since then she has continued to talk to both students and teachers. She has written a book about her findings, and she reports that in contrast to the past, students face enormous pressure to engage in casual sex, particularly in college.

Others contend that while it is common to talk about hooking up, in reality most teens actually have sex as part of a relationship, not as a hookup. The Guttmacher Institute reports that among teens who have had sex, only 16 percent of girls and 28 percent of boys said their first sexual experience was with a casual friend or acquaintance. Instead, 70 percent of females and 56 percent of males said that the first time they had sex it was with a steady partner. Researchers Best and Bogle say these numbers are consistent with their findings that most young people who have sex do so as part of a relationship. They explain that these relationships might be short, with teens breaking up and developing

> "Hookups are simple and do not have to involve romantic feelings. When a hookup ends, people can usually move on, free of any ongoing stress involving the matter."[13]
>
> —Lindsay Nance, editor of the Terra Linda High School newspaper.

a new relationship after a short period of time, but that teens are not just having casual or anonymous sex.

How Teens Feel About Hooking Up

Teens express differing views on how hookups make them feel. Some insist that they prefer hookups because hookups allow them to enjoy sex without having to deal with a relationship. Lindsay Nance, editor of the Terra Linda High School newspaper in San Rafael, California, talks about some of the benefits of hookups: "Hookups are simple and do not have to involve romantic feelings. When a hookup ends, people can usually move on, free of any ongoing stress involving the matter." Nance adds, "Generally, calling a hookup quits is a lot less messy than a relationship. When a relationship ends, tears and heartbreak often ensue because time and emotions have been invested. Hookups tend to carry less of this emotional baggage and allow for the individuals to engage in a form of intimacy without the heartbreak and emotional battles."[13] For all of

A teenage couple snaps a selfie. Experts say that most teens have sex within the context of a committed relationship rather than through casual hookups, although some say they prefer the reduced emotional baggage that accompanies the latter.

these reasons, she believes that many students at her school prefer hookups to relationships.

Freitas disagrees that hookups are fun and stress-free. She insists that "[young people] are acculturated to believe that they are *supposed* to regard sex as a casual, no-big-deal type of experience, yet many of them discover that sex is in fact a big deal."[14] During her research, when she asked students their feelings about sex, many reported that although fellow students often had casual attitudes toward sex, they themselves did not.

Consent Laws

Even though many teens believe that the decision to have sex is a matter of personal choice, teen sex is actually regulated by age-of-consent laws. The age of consent is the age at which a

Sexual Violence

Although research shows that sex is fairly common among teens, it also reveals that a high percentage of teens are subjected to sexual violence, which means kissing, touching, or sex to which they do not consent. For instance, CDC statistics from 2013 reveal that about 7 percent of students have been forced to have sexual intercourse against their will. The agency found that females were more likely than males to report sexual violence. In a study published in 2013 in *JAMA Pediatrics*, researchers reported on their investigation of 1,058 fourteen- to twenty-one-year-olds. They found that almost one in ten had experienced some type of sexual violence. Commenting on this finding, Monica Swahn, an associate director of research with the Emory Center for Injury Control in Atlanta, Georgia, says, "These numbers are very high and also very troubling." Swahn continues, "These are serious forms of victimization with lasting scars, both physically and emotionally." The harms that come from sexual violence can affect a person for the rest of his or her life.

Quoted in Randy Dotinga, "1 in 5 U.S. Teen Girls Physically or Sexually Abused While Dating," HealthDay, March 2, 2015. http://consumer.healthday.com.

person is considered to be legally allowed to consent to having sex. If a person is under the age of consent, even if he or she understands and agrees to sex, that consent is not legally recognized. Under consent laws, an adult who has sex with a teen under the age of consent can be charged with statutory rape, even if the teen agreed to the sexual encounter. These laws have been created because people believe that many teens lack experience and maturity, and as a result they may be unable to fully understand the possible consequences of sex. Most countries have adopted consent laws to protect teens from STDs, pregnancy, and from confusing or abusive relationships (especially involving older, more experienced adults who might coerce a teen into having sex). The age of consent varies worldwide, from about twelve to eighteen. In the United States, age-of-consent laws vary by state but range in age from sixteen to eighteen.

Although age-of-consent laws are intended to protect young people from abusive adults, young teens involved with older teens may run into trouble in connection with these laws. If nobody complains about two underage teens having sex, they are unlikely to be prosecuted by law. However, there have been numerous cases where parents or other adults report a teenage sexual encounter to police, leading to legal consequences for one or both teens. For example, in 2003 seventeen-year-old Genarlow Wilson had oral sex with a consenting fifteen-year-old girl at a New Year's Eve party. After the encounter was caught on videotape, he was sentenced to ten years in prison. Critics argued that his sentence was unfair because consent laws are intended to protect teens from predatory adults, not consensual sex with other teens. The Georgia Supreme Court agreed that the punishment was excessive, later ordering that he be released. The Georgia law was also changed to make consensual sex between teens a misdemeanor punishable by no more than a year in prison. Many other states recognize that sex between two underage teens is usually less of a threat than sex between a teen and an adult. As a result, they have laws that take into account the age gap between the two people having sex and create exceptions or lesser punishments when the participants are close in age. However, some states do not differentiate, and underage teens still risk jail time for having sex.

A Disagreement on the Realities of Teen Sex

Overall, despite all the surveys and research studies that have been done, society continues to disagree about the reality of sex in teenage culture. Some people believe that an increasing number of teens no longer see it as a big deal and that, as a result, irresponsible and promiscuous behavior has become common. Author Nancy Jo Sales spoke with teenagers throughout the United States and found many tales of out-of-control behavior. For example, she heard stories of parties where teenage girls wear practically nothing and engage in sexual activity with multiple partners. One girl told her, "People hook up with more than one person. It's dark and, like, 100 kids are there. It's not considered a big deal. Guys try and hook up with as many girls as possible." This girl also told Sales, "They have lists and stuff. This kid in my grade has this list of 92 girls he's hooked up with."[15] In another interview with Los Angeles teens, Sales reports, "They talked about girls who had made sex tapes; girls who had sex with different guys at parties every weekend."[16] Although many people are shocked to hear such stories, according to Sales and other researchers, such behavior is occurring among an increasing number of teens.

Others, however, argue that while teens do tell sensational stories—such as the ones that Sales heard—most US teens

> "We are seeing teens waiting longer to have sex, using contraceptives more frequently when they start having sex, and being less likely to become pregnant."[17]
>
> —Researcher Lawrence Finer.

are not having sex with dozens of people or making sex tapes; in reality, they are actually becoming more conservative about sex. Lawrence Finer has researched teenage sexual behavior, and he concludes that teens are more responsible about sex than in the past. He says, "Policymakers and the media often sensationalize teen sexual behavior, suggesting that adolescents as young as 10 or 11 are increasingly sexually active. But the data just don't support that concern." Instead, he says, "we are seeing teens waiting longer to have sex, using contraceptives more frequently when they start having sex, and being less likely to become pregnant than their peers of past decades."[17]

Chapter Two

Influences on Teenage Sexual Behavior

John (not his real name) is nineteen years old and has never had sex. He says that he feels enormous pressure to do so though. "In a sense, the message is that you aren't really a man until you've been with a woman," says John. He says that the social pressure he faces regarding sex causes him a lot of stress, explaining, "To me, the word 'sex' brings to mind the emotions of both failure and isolation; failure to act and to be a man, and isolation from my non-virgin friends."[18] In fact, he says he feels so much pressure to lose his virginity that he lies about it to other people, telling his friends that he used to have a girlfriend with whom he had frequent sex. As John's situation illustrates, teenage sexual behavior is usually about more than simply one person choosing how to act. Instead, teenage sexual behavior is influenced by a multitude of factors, including peer pressure, the media, hormones, and even family.

Peer Pressure

Like John, many teens report that peer pressure significantly influences their own sexual behavior and that of their friends. In some cases peer pressure is obvious, such as when a teen like John is told that he needs to have sex in order to be a real man. In other cases, however, it is more subtle, such as when a teen sees that most of his or her friends have had sex and wants to do so in order to be the same as everybody else. Although some teens say that peer pressure keeps them from being sexually active, it is far more likely for teens to engage in various types of sexual activity out of fear of not fitting in. Meg says this is what happened to her: "I was 16 when I lost my virginity. I always felt pressure to have sex as I knew people around me were."[19] Christine had a similar experience. She says, "All the people in school knew I was a virgin and constantly teased me saying I was 'A LITTLE GIRL.' So I did it."[20]

Research shows that peer pressure can also cause teens to have unprotected sex. In 2012 the CDC released a report on teen pregnancy in the United States based on surveys of teens who gave birth between 2004 and 2008. It found that peer pressure played an important role in whether teens used contraception. Of those teens who said they did not use contraception, only a small percentage said they had trouble getting it; it was much more common for them to say that they did not use it because their partner did not want to.

Teens may feel pressure to have sex from their friends and other peers. Many succumb to this pressure in order to feel that they fit in with those around them.

While it has long been recognized that peer pressure is a key factor influencing teen decisions about sex, one recent study shows that what teens *think* their friends are doing sexually may be even more important than what their friends are actually saying or doing. In 2014 researchers reported in the *Personality and Social Psychology Review* on their analysis of how peer pressure works in teens. They analyzed fifty-eight studies that involved thousands of teens in fifteen countries. They found that while peer pressure played a role in decisions about sex, the biggest influence was what teens *thought* their friends were doing. "Adolescents who think that their peers engage in sex are more likely to engage in sex themselves," says lead researcher Daphne van de Bongardt. She adds, "Peers' approval of having sex, or peer pressure to have sex, also matter, but seem to matter less."[21] Van de Bongardt also points out that teens often have misconceptions about what their friends are doing—meaning their decisions about sex might very likely be influenced by false assumptions.

> "Adolescents who think that their peers engage in sex are more likely to engage in sex themselves."[21]
>
> —Researcher Daphne van de Bongardt.

Social Media Influences

Peer pressure to engage in various types of sexual behavior has been amplified by social media. Social media is an important form of communication and socialization for many teens. The majority spend hours a day messaging and posting information, photos, and videos of their lives to various social media accounts. Some of that online activity includes sexual discussions and postings. For example, some teens post provocative photos of themselves or share with their friends the sexual details of their relationships. Some even use social media to engage in sexual activity. Author Nancy Jo Sales explains, "There's Snapchat, where teenagers share pictures of

The prevalence of smartphones among teens makes it easy for them to engage in sexual behavior through social media. This behavior includes posting provocative photos of themselves or sharing sexual details about their relationships.

their bodies or body parts; on Skype, sometimes they strip for each other or masturbate together. On Omegle, they can talk to strangers, and sometimes the talk turns sexual."[22]

Teens report that because they are exposed to so much sexual activity online, they often feel pressured to engage in sexual activity themselves. In 2012 security technology company McAfee surveyed teens on their opinions regarding the way social networking affects their lives. Many teens said that as a result of the popularity of social networking, relationship details have become very public, and there is increased pressure to do what everyone else is doing. One respondent explained, "Everyone (on Facebook) is putting out there what they do with their boyfriends and there is some pressure to do the same."[23] Overall, 46 percent of those teens surveyed said that the Internet influences what their boyfriend or girlfriend expects from them in their relationship.

Physical and Chemical Changes

In addition to peer pressure, the way teens think and act regarding sex is significantly impacted by the physical changes that occur as they develop into adults. The teenage body experiences tremendous physical change. Some of that change continues to occur in the brain until the early to mid-twenties. Much of an individual's judgment and decision making happens in a part of the brain called the frontal lobe—and in teens, the frontal lobe is not fully developed. As the American College of Pediatricians explains, "The frontal lobe, the judgment center or CEO of the brain, allows the individual to contemplate and plan actions, to evaluate consequences of behaviors, to assess risk, and to think strategically. It is also the 'inhibition

Access to Contraception

There is disagreement over how teen sexual activity is impacted by the availability of contraceptives. Some critics argue that when teens are given contraception, they are more likely to have sex. Teacher Kristine Tucker explains, "For some teens—knowing that they aren't at as much risk for sexually transmitted diseases and that pregnancy risks are greatly reduced—birth control encourages promiscuous behavior." Others contend that teen choices about whether to have sex have nothing to do with the availability of contraception. For example, former health worker Maria Newfield says, "Generally speaking, if young people are going to have sex, they will do it whether you give them condoms or not." She adds, "I used to be a sexual health worker and never, ever came across a teenager who said they weren't going to have sex before, but now that their parents/school/clinic gave them contraception they would go for it." Newfield and others in favor of supplying teens with contraceptives insist that doing so simply allows them to have sex more safely.

Kristine Tucker, "Pros and Cons of Giving Birth Control to Teenagers," Livestrong, August 16, 2013. www.live strong.com.

Maria Newfield, commenting on "By Giving Condoms to Our Teen Children, Are We Allowing Them to Have Sex?," Quora. www.quora.com.

center' of the brain, discouraging the individual from acting impulsively."[24] As a result of having an immature frontal lobe, teens are not always able to properly assess a situation and make healthy and appropriate decisions. This increases the likelihood of becoming sexually active without thinking about the consequences.

Teenage sexual behavior is also influenced by hormones. As the body and sexual organs begin to mature during adolescence, hormones are released. Hormones are chemicals that make these changes possible. In addition to helping the body physically mature, hormones also affect moods and emotions. Hormones can cause teenagers to experience strong sexual feelings that they have never had before. They may think about sex a lot, find themselves attracted to other people, and want to have sex. In an online forum, a girl anonymously posted about feeling as though she could not control her sexual thoughts and emotions. She explained, "Lately, I can't stop thinking about sex! I haven't had it. . . . I don't even have a boyfriend, nor do I want one." However, despite that, she said, "I still can't stop thinking about it. Every time I see a boy, I just instinctively imagine what they would look like naked in bed with me." She asked, "What can I do? I'm really stressed out, because I don't want sex and want it at the same time."[25] As her story illustrates, the sexual feelings that come from hormones can be confusing. Although a teen might not want to have sex, his or her body feels many sexual urges.

Drugs and Alcohol

Teen sexual behavior is also influenced by alcohol and drug use. According to the US Department of Health and Human Services, in 2013 almost a quarter of twelve- to twenty-year-olds reported drinking alcohol in the month before the survey. Almost 9 percent used illicit drugs during that same period. Alcohol and drug use lowers inhibitions and can cause poor judgment. This can cause teens to do things they would not do when sober, including participating in sexual activity. Planned Parenthood warns, "Lots of young adults say they've done more sexual stuff after drinking or doing drugs than they'd planned." In addition, it cautions that sexual activity is often more risky while drunk than while sober. It explains, "If you're drunk or high, you might not use condoms correctly, or you might forget to use them at all."[26] This means that having sex after drinking or using drugs increases the risk that a person will become pregnant or contract an STD.

Despite the risks, research reveals that many teens do have sex after drinking or using drugs. A 2013 CDC report, for example, states that among the 34 percent of sexually active students nationwide, almost a quarter drank alcohol or used drugs before their most recent sexual encounter. In a high school newspaper article, a northern California senior says that alcohol and sex are a common combination at her school: "Usually, people get drunk and hook up. They don't know what they are doing and they can't control it."[27]

The Role of Parents

Another important influence on teenage sexual behavior is parents. Research shows that what teens choose to do sexually is strongly influenced by how their parents communicate with them about sex. The National Campaign to Prevent Teen and Unplanned Pregnancy states, "Teens consistently report that parents—not peers, not partners, not popular culture—most influence their decisions about relationships and sex."[28] Unfortunately, research shows that many teens do not receive enough sexual information and guidance from their parents. For a 2012 survey commissioned by Planned Parenthood, *Family Circle* magazine, and the Center for Latino Adolescent and Family Health at New York University, researchers interviewed 1,046 fifteen- to eighteen-year-olds and the same number of parents. While most of the teens and parents said they were talking with each other about sex, discussions often left out important subjects or were infrequent. Planned Parenthood reports, "Parents and teens aren't tackling the tough topics."[29] For example, researchers found that only 29 percent of parents had talked to their teens about birth control, and only 27 percent of teens say that their parents had talked to them often about how to say no to sex.

Research also shows that a family's socioeconomic level can influence teen decision making about sex. Researchers Joel Best and Kathleen A. Bogle have found that teens are less likely to be sexually experienced if their mother is a college graduate, if she had her first child at age twenty or older, and if both parents live in the home. They also found that teens from lower-income families are more likely to have sex at younger ages. Overall, the researchers say, parents are critical to their children's choices about sex: "To be sure, teens make choices. But those choices are shaped both by an individual's location within the larger social structure—by class and ethnicity—and, importantly, by their families. Teens make choices, but their choices are also structured by parental influence."[30]

"Lots of young adults say they've done more sexual stuff after drinking or doing drugs than they'd planned."[26]

—Planned Parenthood.

Media Influences

Some research also suggests that the media help shape teenage beliefs about sex. The film and television industries are often accused of depicting sex as a harmless pastime or a normal part of all teen relationships. Bombarded by such depictions, impressionable young people may come to view sex in much the same way. Author Carolyn C. Ross insists, "Media messages normalize early sexual experimentation and portray sex as casual, unprotected and consequence-free, encouraging sexual activity long before children are emotionally, socially or intellectually ready."[31] There is some research to support this contention. In 2012 researchers reported in *Psychological Science* about their investigation into how sexual content in movies influences teenage sexual behavior. The researchers looked at the sexual content of hundreds of popular movies, then they asked 1,228 twelve- to fourteen-year-olds which movies they had seen. Six years later they surveyed those same participants about their sexual behaviors. They found that teens who were exposed to more sexual content in movies were more likely to start having sex at a younger age, to have more sexual partners, and to be less likely to use condoms with their sexual partners.

However, other researchers contend that the media influence on teenage sexual behavior is minimal. Researchers led by Gert Martin Hald of the University of Copenhagen in Denmark surveyed 4,600 fifteen- to twenty-five-year-olds in the Netherlands. They found that 45 percent of females and 88 percent of males reported viewing sexually explicit material on the Internet, television, and other media in the twelve-month period before the survey. When they investigated the effects of this exposure, they found only a minimal connection between the media images and risky sexual behaviors. Hald says, "Our data suggest that other factors such as personal dispositions—specifically sexual sensation seeking—rather than consumption of sexually explicit material may play a more important role in a range of sexual behaviors of adolescents and young adults."[32] *Sensation seeking* is defined as the tendency for teens to seek novel and intense types of stimulation. Hald advises that sexual activity cannot simply be traced back to media exposure but must be understood in light of other factors, including an individual's personality and preferences.

> "Our data suggest that other factors such as personal dispositions . . . rather than consumption of sexually explicit material may play a more important role in a range of sexual behaviors."[32]
>
> —*Researcher Gert Martin Hald.*

Teen Pregnancy on Television

Sexually suggestive media images are not the only area of concern in terms of influencing teen choices about sex. In recent years a number of television shows and movies have been created specifically to focus on teen pregnancy and parenting. There is heated debate over how these shows affect teens. Most well known are MTV's *16 and Pregnant* and *Teen Mom*, reality shows that follow pregnant teenagers and teenage mothers as they go about their daily lives. These shows are popular with MTV viewers; according to a 2014 *New York Times* article, some episodes have attracted more than 3 million viewers.

Advocates of these shows insist that they deter risky sexual behavior because they help teens understand the difficulties of pregnancy and teen parenting. "Watching 'Teen Mom,' you're close to the characters," explains high school student Kendall Schutzer. "You're watching them go through their day. You're seeing what different aspects of life are like with a child. I don't know how else you could get to know something like that."[33]

The MTV reality show Teen Mom *starred Kailyn Lowry, Jenelle Evans, Leah Messer-Calvert, and Chelsea Houska, among others. The show followed the teenage mothers as they went about their daily lives. Observers disagree fiercely over whether such reality shows discourage teen parenting by depicting its difficulties, or encourage it by glamorizing it and making it seem desirable.*

Texting About Sex

Most teenagers rely heavily on their cell phone and other electronic media to communicate with one another and to access information. While critics worry that such technology can make risky sexual behavior such as sexting possible, some research has shown that electronic media can actually have a beneficial impact on the sex lives of teens. In 2014 researchers reported in the *Journal of Adolescent Health* about how young people use texting and other types of electronic communication to talk about sexual topics. They studied 176 US high school juniors and seniors and found that this electronic communication actually seems to have a positive impact. For example, they found that students who talked about birth control by text or other technology were almost four times more likely to use a condom when they had sex. Laura Widman, lead author of the study, stresses that the electronic conversations teens have about sex do not just consist of sexting. They include discussions that help them learn important information, such as how to be safe. She theorizes that electronic communication might encourage students to talk about these topics because it can be less embarrassing than face-to-face communication. "It's not all about risky behavior," she says. "It might be another way that teens can have these conversations that can be a little bit awkward."

Quoted in Ronnie Cohen, "Teens Who Text About Condoms More Likely to Use Them," Reuters, February 19, 2014. www.reuters.com.

In 2010 the National Campaign to Prevent Teen and Unplanned Pregnancy studied *16 and Pregnant* and found that, in addition to helping teens understand these issues, it encouraged them to talk about what they had seen on the show. Researchers found that more than a third of those teens who watched the show talked about it afterward to a parent, and a third discussed it with a sibling, boyfriend, or girlfriend. They found that when teens talked about the show, they were less likely to believe that pregnancy is something that most teens want. In 2014 a report was released by the National Bureau of Economic Research that also concluded that *16 and Pregnant* increased communication about sex-related topics. Researchers found that the show led to more social media postings and Internet searches on abortion and contraception. They also found that in the eighteen months following the introduction of the show, there was a 5.7 percent reduction in teen births.

However, critics contend that shows like *16 and Pregnant* actually encourage teen pregnancy and parenting by glamorizing it and making it seem desirable to teens. In 2014 Indiana University researchers found that teens who watched the show were more likely to have an unrealistic perception of what it is like to be a teenage parent. They report that teens who spend a lot of time watching the show are more likely to believe that teen parents have a high income and an enviable quality of life. "The fact that teens in the study seemed to think that being a teen parent was easy might increase the likelihood that they'll engage in unsafe sexual practices," explains researcher Nicole Martins, "because that's not a real consequence to them."[34] The researchers believe that the show may glamorize teen parenting so much that teens ultimately see it as a good thing, despite all the problems that the show's stars struggle with. They state, "The attention and opportunities seemingly thrown at these teen parents may appear so appealing to viewers that no amount of horror stories from the reality shows themselves can override them."[35]

Pornography

In addition to learning about sex on television and in movies, a substantial number of teens are exposed to sexual content through pornography. The Internet has made it easy to access such content, either accidentally or intentionally. There is disagreement about how it affects teens. Many people believe that viewing pornography is extremely harmful to young people because it shows sex in an unrealistic and often unhealthy manner. Connie, who teaches health education to fifth- and sixth-graders, reports that many of the boys in her classes say that they have seen Internet pornography. She believes it is teaching them unhealthy lessons about sex, such as that sex has no relation to emotions or caring. She recalls a student's comment after a lesson in which she explained that sex is an expression of deep affection between two people. A boy named Gabe challenged this description, saying "Well, I think you *don't* need to like the person. I saw sex on the Internet. My cousin showed me. They just do it 'cause it's fun, they like it."[36] In reality, sex does involve emotions and often has serious consequences. However, pornography usually does not show this side of sexuality—and critics worry that teens who have repeated exposure to pornography will come to accept sex as a shallow, casual act.

Although many people agree that pornography is harmful to teens, scientific proof for this view is hard to come by. In 2013 the Office of the Children's Commissioner for England released a report about the impact of pornography on young people. Researchers reviewed existing research on the topic and found that a significant proportion of young people have viewed pornography. They also found evidence that pornography affects their sexual beliefs. However, the researchers admitted that they were unable to make definite conclusions about exactly how young people are affected and how long the effects last. They concluded that more research is needed. American researcher Eric Owens also reviewed existing research and came to a similar conclusion. "By the end we looked at 40 to 50 studies," says Owens, "and it became, 'O.K., this one tells us A, this one tells us B.' To some degree we threw up our hands and said, there is no conclusion to be drawn here."[37] It is very difficult to actually conduct research about how pornography affects teens. Researchers can ask teens about whether they have viewed it, but it would be unethical to actually expose teens to pornography in order to study the result.

Overall, the choices that teens make about sex are influenced by many factors. Some of these influences are extremely powerful, such as peer pressure. Many of them are inescapable, such as the hormones that flood the teenage body during adolescence. By understanding all of the factors that are influencing them, teens can make better choices about what decisions to make.

Chapter Three

The Consequences of Sexual Activity by Teens

Maggie (not her real name) had sex with her boyfriend and became pregnant at age fourteen. She says that she was shocked to find out she was pregnant. "I still remember my first OB/GYN appointment," she says. "The first thing the doctor said to me was, 'Congratulations.' I just stared at her, dumbfounded." Maggie explains that pregnancy completely altered her life, forcing her to deal with many emotions and responsibilities for which she was not ready. She says, "I was so young and had so much more to do. But I pushed everything aside to take care of my child, even if I was just a child myself." As her story shows, sex can have significant consequences. Maggie's advice to other teens is not to have sex until they understand all these potential consequences and are ready to deal with them. She advises, "Wait until you feel you're really mature enough to handle the emotions and outcomes of sex. I was only 14. I was definitely not ready for all the responsibility that sex brought me."[38] Pregnancy is just one of the possible outcomes of teen sex. Having sex can be an intense emotional experience, can alter a person's reputation, and also comes with the risk of STDs.

Emotional Effects

Sexual activity is one of the most intimate acts between two people. As a result, it can provoke strong feelings and significantly change the way teens feel about each other and about themselves. Matt Posner, coauthor of the *Teen Guide to Sex & Relationships,* warns that teens thinking about engaging in sexual activity need to realize that there will be emotional consequences, and they should be ready to deal with them. He cautions, "Your body tells you to have sex, because your body is ready to make babies, but it's not just your body that matters. Your feelings and thoughts need to be ready too."[39]

Some teens report that sex is an emotionally rewarding experience, making them feel happy and close to their partner. For example, fifteen-year-old Kate says, "My boyfriend and I have been together for six months and we are in love. We have a great relationship with excellent communication, and we made the decision to have sex." She says that sex has been an extremely positive experience that has strengthened their relationship. She continues, "I have a bright future and sex is not going to corrupt that, because sex is meant to be a positive, intimate experience that bonds couples and is healthy."[40] She says that sex has been a beautiful thing in her relationship.

> "Your body tells you to have sex, because your body is ready to make babies, but it's not just your body that matters. Your feelings and thoughts need to be ready too."[39]
>
> —Author Matt Posner.

However, not all teens feel happy and fulfilled after having sex. Some report that they strongly regret their choice or that they feel used or guilty. For this reason, some teens choose not to have sex. For instance, eighteen-year-old Brooke says that she has enough to worry about emotionally without adding the intense emotions that come with sex. She explains, "Quite honestly, as a girl whose hormones rage for a good week every other month or so, the last thing I need to worry about is sex. Why get so emotionally and intimately attached with someone who most likely won't be with you (or maybe even remember you) a week, maybe a month down the road?"[41] At this stage in her life, the teenager says, sex seems like more pain than gain; she has decided that it is not worth the trouble, and she plans to wait until she is married.

Reputation

Sex can also have a dramatic impact on a teen's reputation. Research shows that this impact is typically very different for boys and girls; whereas girls are often shamed, boys are often congratulated for having sex. *Teen Vogue* writer Rachel Simmons tells the story of eighteen-year-old Zoe to illustrate these differences. She says that Zoe began dating a guy at her school, and then someone started a rumor that the two were having sex and doing drugs. Even though this was false, people began to treat Zoe very differently because they thought she was having sex. They started whispering about her behind her

An Addiction to Risky Sexual Behavior

Researchers have found that because of the way their brains are still developing, it is common for teens to take risks. This includes taking sexual risks, such as having sex with lots of people or without contraception. Unfortunately, there is some evidence that when teens participate in a lot of risky sexual behavior, this might actually change the way their brains develop, causing them to become addicted to such behavior. The American College of Pediatricians explains that this is because the brain undergoes enormous change during the teen years: "Between 11 and 13 years of age, the adolescent's brain experiences rapid growth of nerve cells, along with increased numbers of connections between nerves (synapses)." In addition, it says, "this growth is followed by a time of 'pruning,' when nerve cells that are not used or needed are deprived of nutrition and die. The pruning process allows the adolescent brain to function more rapidly for tasks that are already known, but decreases the brain's capacity to learn new tasks or acquire new skills." It explains that the connections that develop and the pruning that occurs are greatly influenced by what a teen does. Therefore, if a young person engages in a lot of risky sexual behavior, his or her brain can actually become wired to keep behaving this way.

American College of Pediatricians, "The Teenage Brain: Under Construction," May 2011. www.acpeds.org.

back. Zoe says, "I couldn't walk around campus without being called 'whore.'" In contrast, Zoe's boyfriend was congratulated by other students. "We would walk into the common room and people would start clapping and bow down to him," Zoe says. "It was like, 'Yeah! You scored! That rules!'"[42]

Research shows that experiences such as Zoe's are common across the United States. High school counselor Julia V. Taylor maintains that a double standard often exists for teenage boys and girls when it comes to sexual behavior. "Unfortunately, the notion of 'she's a slut, he's a stud' still rings loud and clear in the halls of schools everywhere," she explains. "Girls can make one wrong move and be branded a slut forever. Guys can be labeled a player for similar behavior. It's a badge of honor in the eyes of his guy friends."[43]

Pregnancy can result in even more dramatic changes to the way a teen is treated by peers. In 2011 seventeen-year-old Washington teenager Gaby Rodriguez faked being pregnant—even keeping the truth from some of her own family members—as an experiment for her senior project. She wanted to see how people would treat her when they thought she was pregnant. In a book she wrote about the experiment, Rodriguez says that her peers constantly stared at her and whispered about her. She says, "I'd see a group of girls purposely not making eye contact with me, just shaking their heads in judgment and gossiping with each other as I came near." She says that all the negative attention she received was difficult to deal with, stating, "I wanted to hide. It was exhausting feeling like people were judging me all day."[44] Rodriguez says that some days she went home and cried and wished that she had never decided to do this experiment.

Sexually Transmitted Diseases

When a person engages in sexual activity, he or she risks more than emotions and reputation, however. Sexual contact can result in STDs, also called sexually transmitted infections. STDs are most commonly transmitted through sexual intercourse, but a person can also get an STD by putting his or her hands, mouth, or genitals on the genitals of a person who is infected. The list of STDs is long and ranges from relatively mild infections, such as pubic lice, to life-threatening illnesses such as HIV/AIDS. They are transmitted through both homosexual and heterosexual intercourse. Some STDs are caused by bacteria and are curable, usually with antibiotics. Others are caused by viruses and cannot be cured. If a person is treated for an STD and it goes away, they can still catch it again through sex with an infected person.

It is impossible to know for sure whether a person has an STD simply by looking at him or her; often, an infected person has no symptoms. However, he or she can still infect another person through sexual contact. This is what happened to seventeen-year-old Amber after she had sex with her boyfriend, Sean. Amber says, "I didn't notice anything on his body that was unusual or that looked suspicious, so I wasn't worried. Turns out I should have been, because a few days later, I had a couple of small, hard sores. They didn't hurt, but they didn't go away."[45] After getting tested, she discovered she had syphilis. According to Amber, her boyfriend did not even know he had the illness. She explains that Sean had also gotten sores and rashes after he had sex with a previous girlfriend, but these problems eventually disappeared, so he thought he was okay. Even if a person has no symptoms, as in Sean's case, he or she can still suffer serious health problems from an STD. Testing is the only way to be sure about whether a person has an STD.

> "Girls can make one wrong move and be branded a slut forever. Guys can be labeled a player for similar behavior."[43]
>
> —High school counselor Julia V. Taylor.

STDs affect teens at a disproportionally high rate. According to the CDC, every year approximately 20 million new STD infections occur in the United States, and almost half of them are among fifteen- to twenty-five-year-olds. The US Department of Health and Human Services stresses that young women face the greatest risk from these illnesses. It warns, "Today, four in 10 sexually active teen girls have had an STD that can cause infertility and even death."[46]

Common Bacterial STDs

Some of the most serious bacterial STDs are chlamydia, gonorrhea, and syphilis. Chlamydia can infect the penis, vagina, cervix, rectum, urethra, throat, or eyes. In some people, symptoms include discharge from the penis or vagina, painful urination, or pain during sex. For many people, however, this infection has no symptoms; 70 to 95 percent of women and 90 percent of men have no symptoms, according to Planned Parenthood. For this reason, chlamydia is sometimes referred to as the *silent disease*. If chlamydia is left untreated for a long time, it can cause serious damage to the reproductive system, including infertility. When diagnosed, it is easily treated with antibiotics.

Young people age fifteen to twenty-five account for nearly half of the new cases of sexually transmitted diseases (STDs) reported each year. One such STD is syphilis, whose second-stage symptoms include a rash that does not itch (pictured).

Gonorrhea can infect the genitals, rectum, or throat. Some people experience no symptoms; others, however, may have discharge from the penis or vagina or experience painful urination. Women may experience menstrual irregularity, fever, and abdominal pain. Like chlamydia, gonorrhea can be treated with antibiotics, but untreated gonorrhea can damage the reproductive system.

The potential symptoms of syphilis include a painless sore or an open ulcer called a chancre, body rashes, fever, swollen glands, and muscle pains. The CDC says many people may not realize they have syphilis because its symptoms often resemble those of other illnesses. It explains,

> "Today, four in 10 sexually active teen girls have had an STD that can cause infertility and even death."[46]
>
> *—The US Department of Health and Human Services.*

> Syphilis has been called "the great imitator" because it has so many possible symptoms, many of which look like symptoms from other diseases. The painless syphilis sore that you would get after you are first infected can be confused for an ingrown hair, zipper cut, or other seemingly harmless bump. The non-itchy body rash that develops during the second stage of syphilis can show up on the palms of your hands and soles of your feet, all over your body, or in just a few places.[47]

Syphilis can be effectively treated in its early stages, but untreated syphilis can eventually cause damage to the nervous system, heart, or brain, and even cause death.

Common Viral STDs

The most serious viral STDs that teens get from sex are human papillomavirus (HPV), herpes, and HIV/AIDs. HPV is the most common STD among teens and among the US population in general, according to the CDC. In fact, the agency reports that almost every sexually active person in the United

States will get HPV at some point in his or her life. In many cases, HPV has no symptoms and causes no harm, and it goes away by itself. However, for some people it causes genital warts and cervical or other types of cancer. There is no way to cure HPV once a person gets it, but a vaccine is available to prevent this STD and is given as a series of three shots. Although the vaccine is optional in the United States, the CDC recommends that all young people receive it starting at about age twelve.

Herpes is a virus that causes outbreaks of blisters around the genitals, mouth, or rectum. These blisters break open and can be very painful and take weeks to heal. The first time a person has a herpes outbreak, he or she may also have flu-like symptoms such as a fever or body aches. Commenting on an article about living with herpes, one teen explains just how unpleasant it can be. She says, "I'm a 15 yr old girl with genital herpes. I found out that I had it about 3 months ago, when I had my first outbreak. It was SO PAINFUL. I couldn't walk whatsoever, couldn't pee, or anything. . . . It sucks knowing that I'm only 15 and have this for the rest of my life."[48] While there is no cure for herpes, there are medicines that can prevent or shorten outbreaks.

The most serious STD is HIV. HIV damages the body's immune system, meaning the body loses its ability to fight off infections and disease. Over time the infection causes so much harm that AIDS develops. In the recent past, HIV infections nearly always developed into AIDS, and AIDS was nearly always fatal. Now, however, drug treatments can dramatically prolong the lives of people with HIV and prevent them from developing AIDS. Even with treatment, living with HIV can be difficult; the medications often have unpleasant side effects such as fatigue, nausea, and hallucinations. Mike, who suffers from HIV, talks about when he started his medication:

[I had] dreams so vivid I would wake up in the middle of the night and it would take me a few moments to try to figure out where I was, what was happening. I once found myself in the closet crying with my favorite sweater in hand, crying because I believed it was infested with bedbugs and I would have to throw it out. I actually washed it afterwards so I would be able to calm down and able to return to sleep.[49]

When a person has HIV, he or she can never have sex or have a baby without the risk of passing the illness along to partners or children.

The herpes virus causes painful blisters around the mouth, genitals, and rectum, as well as flu-like symptoms. Although there is no cure for the disease, medicines exist that can prevent or shorten outbreaks.

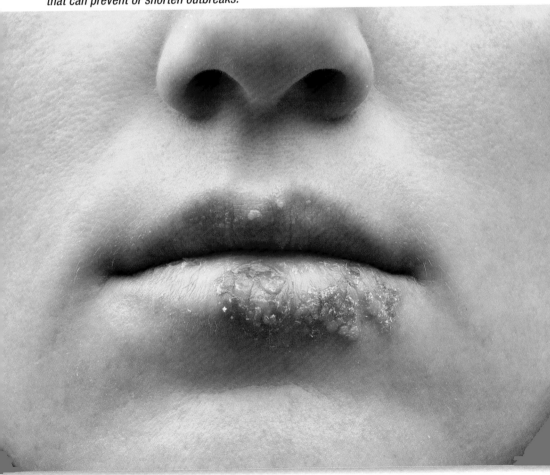

Pregnancy

Although the risk of STDs gets significant attention in discussions about sexually active teens, no outcome brings as much concern as teen pregnancy. While some teen parents have a positive experience, the majority struggle financially and emotionally to deal with being a parent and caring for a child. Most teens have absolutely no idea how hard it is to raise a child. Lauren Dolgen, creator of the television shows *16 and Pregnant* and *Teen Mom*, says,

> It's not a fairy tale where every girl ends up with the American dream—a loving husband, a white picket fence and the career they've always hoped for. These young women struggle to make ends meet. They make mistakes as they try to navigate an adult life too soon. Relationships with their partners, parents and friends often crumble, and the pressure of raising a child is often too much to bear.[50]

Caring for a baby is a responsibility that most teens are completely unprepared for. Teen parents, especially mothers, struggle emotionally and financially. According to one study, about half of teen mothers lived with income levels below the poverty line.

Numerous stories from teen parents confirm this harsh reality. For instance, teenage father Nate says that instead of going to college and playing football like he wanted to, he was forced to take a job at a pork-packing plant in his hometown in Indiana in order to support his girlfriend and their soon-to-be-born baby. He explains that even with this job, he is just scraping by. "It's scary," he says, "not having enough money, having no car, to where I feel like I won't be able to provide for both."[51]

> "The educational challenges faced by teen mothers often set the stage for a cycle of economic hardship that repeats across generations."[52]
>
> —The National Campaign to Prevent Teen and Unplanned Pregnancy.

Looking after a baby takes so much time and energy that many teenage parents do not finish high school. As a result of having a limited education, it is more difficult to find a good job, and they are much more likely to live in poverty. The National Campaign to Prevent Teen and Unplanned Pregnancy reports that only about half of teen mothers receive a high school diploma by the time they are twenty-two, compared to 89 percent of teens who do not have a baby. It says that between 2009 and 2010 about 48 percent of teen mothers lived with income levels below the poverty line. When teens become parents, their children are also less likely to do well in school or to finish high school, and so they too are more likely to live in poverty. "The educational challenges faced by teen mothers often set the stage for a cycle of economic hardship that repeats across generations,"[52] says the National Campaign. Teen mothers face a particularly difficult time. They often end up being the one that takes responsibility for looking after the child. Most teen mothers are not married when they give birth. Although fathers are required to help with child support, the National Campaign reports that most teen mothers receive none or very little.

Not only does teen pregnancy often cause emotional and financial problems for parents, it can also be harmful to the baby. Babies born to teens are more likely to be born prematurely or to be born small. Researchers at the National Center for

Teen Dads

While discussions about teen pregnancy typically focus on teen mothers, pregnancy can be very hard on teen dads too. May teen dads report that they find it extremely difficult to deal with the stresses of being a parent. Justin explains how pregnancy turned his life into an emotional roller coaster. He explains that having a baby was very stressful for him and his girlfriend. The couple fought a lot; they broke up and got back together several times. "After our son was born," he says, "we were back to being the perfect couple again until we had a huge disagreement about the health of our son. This led to Child Protective Services and the cops being called." Later, he says, they made up but then broke up yet again. "Every day is a constant struggle," he adds.

Teen father Robert Aleman also describes feelings of guilt because his child is not living with both parents. He says, "I brought him into a world where he doesn't have his parents together. I brought him into a world where he's having to switch homes every other week." Aleman says he wishes that his son had been born later in his life, when he was ready to be a good father.

Justin, "Glimmering Hope," ReachOut.com. http://us.reachout.com.

Quoted in Sharon Jayson, "Teen Parents Talk Legal, Financial Consequences of Sex," *USA Today*, December 14, 2010. http://usatoday30.usatoday.com.

Health Statistics say that almost 15 percent of babies born to fifteen- to seventeen-year-olds are born prematurely. It explains that premature birth among teens has harmful repercussions: "Elevated rates of low birthweight and preterm birth place the infants at greater risk of serious and long-term illness, developmental delays, and of dying in the first year of life."[53] They report that infant mortality rates are much higher for babies born to teen mothers than to adults.

Far-Reaching Consequences

Finally, teen pregnancy also has substantial economic costs for society. According to the CDC, in 2011 teen pregnancy and childbirth cost US taxpayers about $9.4 billion. This includes the cost of health care since teen pregnancy is more likely to result in health problems to both mothers and children. It also includes foster care for unwanted children and lost tax revenue due to the lower education and income of both teen mothers and their children. In addition, the CDC reports that children of teen parents are more likely to incur costs to the criminal justice system because they are more likely to be incarcerated at some time during their lives. As a result of all these costs, reducing teen pregnancy is an important goal for the United States.

Some teens think that sexual activity is not a big deal. What they fail to consider is that sex can have strong emotional effects, can alter reputations, and can have long-lasting consequences for health and well-being—and not just for the two people involved. On Quora, a website where people can post questions and answers on various topics, an anonymous writer explains that teens need to be aware of these effects so they can make good choices about whether to engage in sexual activity. "Sex is a wonderful experience in the right circumstances," the writer states. "It feels good. It heightens your bond with your partner. You learn about your body and have the opportunity to explore someone else's." However, the writer warns, "There are also concerns and consequences that you need to be sure you're ready to deal with. Not just pregnancy and STDs but the emotional toll of possibly doing something that you weren't ready for because of outside pressure. You will have plenty of opportunities in your life to have sex, choose the one that feels right to you."[54]

Chapter Four

Social Efforts to Change Teen Sexual Activity

Numerous public and private efforts are under way in the United States to influence teenage sexual behavior. Research shows that such efforts are needed. The United States has one of the highest teen birthrates in the developed world. According to the National Campaign to Prevent Teen and Unplanned Pregnancy, about three in ten US teenage girls will become pregnant before age twenty. The organization reports that the teen birthrate in the United States is almost one and a half times higher than the United Kingdom's, twice as high as Canada's, and almost ten times higher than Switzerland's. The United States also has a high rate of STD infections among teens.

While many people agree that teen pregnancy and STDs are undesirable, getting teens to make different choices is a challenge. One factor that complicates any efforts to accomplish this goal is the lack of public consensus. There is significant disagreement about exactly what teenage sexual education should consist of and how that education should be accomplished.

Sex Education in Schools

Research shows that most people agree teens should receive some type of sex education in school. As the Sexuality Information and Education Council of the United States (SIECUS) explains, schools have the power to greatly influence young people. It says, "Across the country, schools have direct contact with more than 56 million students for at least 6 hours a day during 13 key years of their development. After the family home, schools are the primary places responsible for the development of young people."[55] Most people believe that schools should use their significant influence to help educate young people about sexuality and safe sexual behavior.

Evidence suggests that teens who receive sex education in school are more likely to make good choices and less likely to engage in harmful or risky sexual behavior. For instance, in 2012 researchers from the Guttmacher Institute reported on a survey of 4,691 fifteen- to twenty-four-year-olds. They found that those teens who received any type of formal sex education waited longer to have sex. They also found that when those teens did have sex, they were more likely to use contraception.

In contrast, teens who do not have sex education at school are more likely to engage in risky sexual activity. This can be seen in Mississippi, a state that did not require schools to provide sex education before 2011. In a 2014 report that looked at the period before the law was changed, SIECUS states that Mississippi students were more likely to have unsafe sex than

Schools are an important source of information for young people regarding sexual topics. Studies have shown that teens who receive formal sex education in school are less likely to engage in harmful or risky behavior than teens who do not.

students in states that offered sex education. It also found that the rates of STDs and pregnancy were higher among Mississippi teens than in the rest of the country. For example, SIECUS reports that in 2011 Mississippi ranked second (behind Arkansas) in teen pregnancies, teen births, and gonorrhea and chlamydia infections. SIECUS also found that Mississippi teens were more likely to have sex at a young age. For instance, they were more than twice as likely as the average US teen to have sex before age thirteen. As a result of strong evidence that sex education in schools is beneficial, many public schools do provide some type of sex education, and in some states it is required by law. According to the National Conference of State Legislatures, as of the beginning of 2015, twenty-two states and the District of Columbia require sex education in public schools. Thirty-three states and the District of Columbia require education about HIV/AIDS. However, the content of sex education can differ substantially. Some schools provide abstinence-only education, which means teaching teens to abstain from sex until they are older. Abstinence-only education does not include any information about contraception. Other schools provide comprehensive sex education. Comprehensive education also encourages teens to wait until they are older to have sex but also gives them information about contraception.

Comprehensive Sex Education

Advocates of comprehensive sex education argue that some teens are going to experiment with sex even if they are taught to abstain. The story of Beth Leyba illustrates this reality. She became sexually active as a teenager despite her plans to wait until marriage. She even wore a purity ring that expressed her commitment to wait. However, she says that like many of her friends, she found abstinence too difficult. Leyba explains, "As all humans are wont to do, I found myself in a romantic relationship that became more and more physical over time. My boyfriend and I were dating for a year before we allowed things to get too hot and heavy one day."[56] Leyba had not received any education about how to be safe in the event that she did have sex—with the result that she became pregnant.

Stories such as Lebya's are common. Thus, advocates insist that it is essential to teach teens how to have sex safely—meaning how to avoid pregnancy and transmission of STDs. Doctoral candidate Jessica Bol analyzed data about the sexual behavior of thousands of teens in the United States in order to better understand what causes them to engage in risky sexual

The Importance of Understanding Consent

In order to build healthy relationships, teens need to learn about consent. The term *consent* means that sexual activity should take place only with the agreement of both partners. Nobody should be pressured or forced into sexual activity. Some experts report that much US sex education does not adequately teach consent. Nora Gelperin of Answer, a national sexuality education organization, explains that because teachers have a limited amount of time to teach sex education classes, they can include only a limited number of topics. She explains, "Unfortunately, it tends to be that teachers focus on what they see as the core content, which is generally pregnancy prevention and STD/HIV prevention." Gelperin says that consent is usually left out.

Kelvin Ayora, a staff writer for the website Sex, Etc., argues that it is vital that youth learn about consent so that they will be able to avoid abusive relationships or other problems later in life. He says, "If we are taught from early on that partners don't owe each other sex and that consent is absolutely necessary, we are better prepared to call out our friends' or classmates' sexist and misogynistic language and behavior." When teens learn about consent, they realize that in a healthy relationship any sexual activity should happen only with the consent of both partners.

Quoted in Lane Florsheim, "If College Students Can't Say What 'Consent' Is, Then We Should Teach It Sooner," *New Republic*, November 7, 2013. www.newrepublic.com.

Kelvin Ayora, "How Comprehensive Sex Ed Can Address Violence Against Women," Sex, Etc., October 6, 2014. http://sexetc.org.

behavior. She concluded that comprehensive sex education leads to safer teen sex practices. She says, "Providing adolescents with sex knowledge and access to birth control is an important preventative intervention. This research found that teens who possess higher levels of sex knowledge and access to contraception are more likely to have protected sex."[57]

Jenelle Marie, founder of the award-winning website the STD Project, interviewed a young woman from South Carolina who contracted herpes through oral sex when she was nineteen years old. The young woman believes that she would never have gotten this disease if she had received comprehensive sex education in school. She stresses that she respected her teachers and listened to what they told her; if they had taught her how to avoid STDs, she would have followed their advice. Instead, she contracted an STD from oral sex. "We weren't told about that stuff," she says. "Sex ed was literally a bunch of kids giggling about gross slides and our teacher telling us not to do it."[58]

> "We vaccinate when kids are little, we teach drivers ed before you get behind the wheel of a car and just like any other prevention, sex-ed needs to happen before sex."[59]
>
> —Kara Ratajczak, a community health educator.

Advocates of comprehensive sex education argue that society should see it as a kind of vaccination against unsafe sexual behavior. Kara Ratajczak is a community health educator for Planned Parenthood of South Florida and the Treasure Coast. She maintains that children should receive comprehensive information about sex starting well before they reach the age when they might actually have sex. "Just like any other prevention, it should be before exposure happens," Ratajczak explains. She points out that society takes preventative action to reduce other types of potential harms to young people: "We vaccinate when kids are little, we teach drivers ed before you get behind the wheel of a car and just like any other prevention, sex-ed needs to happen before sex."[59] In Ratajczak's opinion, comprehensive sex education is a similarly prudent preventive measure.

Abstinence-Only Education

Advocates of abstinence-only education contend that no matter what education they receive, teens are simply not mature enough to make good choices about sex or to handle the potential consequences. A teen pregnancy prevention report released in 2012 by the US House of Representatives argues that is unrealistic to expect teens to make good choices about

Abstinence-only sex education focuses on teaching teens that they should not engage in sexual activity. Proponents of this approach reason that because teens should not be having sex at all, they should not be taught about contraception because such teachings give them a green light to have sex as long as they do so safely.

sex simply because they have attended sex education class-es. The decision to become sexually active is more emotional than rational, so having more knowledge does not necessarily lead to good choices. The House members maintain that teens need to be taught to avoid sexual behavior altogether. They insist, "An abstinence choice ensures that teens will avoid risky sexual behavior that they are not prepared to handle."[60]

While those in favor of comprehensive sex education be-lieve that some teens will have sex no matter what, advocates of abstinence-only education insist that society should refuse to see teen sex as inevitable. The National Abstinence Educa-tion Association argues that teen sex is actually a public health risk because it so often causes pregnancy and STDs. Thus, for the good of society, teen sexual activity needs to be prevented. The organization maintains that just as society continues its ef-forts to reduce other health risks, such as smoking and obesity (even though people continue to smoke and overeat), it should do everything possible to get young people to not engage in sexual activity. It insists, "The fact that many individuals have sex before marriage . . . [does not] mean we should abandon the goal of changing the cultural norm for this behavior."[61]

Advocates of abstinence education also argue that in order to be effective, abstinence education cannot include informa-tion about contraception. They explain that by teaching teens about contraception, society is giving them the message that it is okay for them to have sex if they do so safely. Instead, they contend that teens need to receive a strong, consistent mes-sage that abstinence is the only option.

Virginity Pledges

In addition to abstinence-only education in schools, another way society has tried to encourage teens to remain abstinent is through virginity pledges. A virginity pledge is when a teen pledg-es not to have sex until after he or she marries. Some research has shown that when teens wait to have sex until they are in a committed and stable relationship, their relationships are much stronger overall. One study that appeared in the *Journal of Fam-*

Changing Age-of-Consent Laws

Age-of-consent laws are intended to protect teens from abusive sexual relationships with adults. However, these laws can also criminalize sex between consenting teens. Some critics believe this actually increases the chances that young people will make bad choices about sex. It is argued that when teen sex is against the law, teens are often secretive about their sexual behavior in order to avoid legal consequences. As a result, they are less likely to ask for guidance about important topics such STDs or contraception, and the resulting lack of knowledge increases the chance that they will make bad choices about their sexual behavior. Bioethicist Jacob M. Appel explains,

> Statutes criminalizing . . . [teen sex] are far more likely to harm teenagers than to help them—whether by denying them access to necessary information, deterring them from sharing their experiences with teachers and counselors for fear that they or their partners will be reported to authorities, or driving them to have sex in parked cars and dark alleys rather than safe, warm bedrooms.

Critics of age-of-consent laws insist that these laws should be changed so that sex between two teenagers is not against the law. They hope that by decriminalizing teen sex, society can encourage teens to be more open about their sexual behavior and concerns. As a result, they believe that teens will be better equipped to make good choices about sex.

Jacob M. Appel, "Embracing Teenage Sexuality: Let's Rethink the Age of Consent," *Huffington Post*, March 18, 2010. www.huffingtonpost.com.

ily Psychology, for instance, found that couples who wait until they are married to have sex report a higher level of relationship satisfaction and stability, better communication, and better sex. Sociologist Mark Regnerus of the University of Texas, Austin, explains that having sex too soon can actually weaken a relationship. He says, "Couples who hit the honeymoon too early—that is, prioritize sex promptly at the outset of a relationship—often find their relationships underdeveloped when it comes to the qualities that make relationships stable and spouses reliable and trustworthy."[62]

Virginity pledges draw mixed responses. On the one hand, they are seen as helping young people stick to their values and wait until they are older and more sexually mature before becoming sexually active. On the other hand, they are viewed as detrimental to developing a healthy attitude about sexuality. Critics argue that virginity pledges condition teens to see sex exclusively as a bad thing that they need to avoid. As a result, when they are finally ready to have sex, they struggle to embrace it as a normal and pleasurable part of a committed relationship. Samantha Pugsley took a virginity pledge and remained a virgin until marriage. However, she says that this pledge made her see sex as something dirty; as a result, when she finally married and was ready to have a sexual relationship with her husband, she did not know how to do so in a healthy manner. Pugsley explains, "Waiting didn't give me a happily ever after. Instead, it controlled my identity for over a decade, landed me in therapy, and left me a stranger in my own skin. I was so completely ashamed of my body and my sexuality that it made having sex a demoralizing experience."[63]

Researcher Sarah Diefendorf studied a group of men in their late teens and early twenties who had made virginity pledges and were part of a support group to help them stay virgins until they got married. She interviewed them three times over the course of four years. She also found that virginity pledges led to difficulty later having a healthy sexual relationship because the men were so used to thinking about sex only as something negative.

Encouraging Parental Involvement

Most people believe that school is not the only place teens should learn about sex. Experts on teen sexual behavior report that parents exert a powerful influence on the behaviors and actions of their children regarding sex. They insist that because parents have so much power, the best way to change teen sexual behavior in the United States is for parents to take a more active role in educating their teens about sex and listening to their concerns. Research shows, however, that most parents do not speak frequently and openly to their children about sex. Sinikka Elliott, an assistant professor of sociology at North Carolina State University, interviewed almost fifty parents of teenagers and wrote a book about her findings. She consistently found that although many teens are having sex, a large number of parents refuse to believe that their children are doing so. Elliott says, "Almost all insist that their children are not sexual. Other teenagers may be sexual, even hypersexual, engaging in risky and promiscuous sexual behavior, but their own children, regardless of their age or actual behavior, are 'not that kind of kid.'"[64] Because they refuse to accept that their own children might be having sex or thinking about having sex, many parents do not discuss this topic with their children.

> "How *can* you have a good sexual relationship when no one ever tells you how to do that?"[68]
>
> —Al Vernacchio, a high school sex educator.

Gabby LaRue says that her parents did not teach her anything about sex, leaving her to figure everything out by herself, and she believes this made her life much more complicated than it could have been otherwise. For instance, she tells the story of how she lost her virginity in a closet at a party, to a guy she did not even like. She says, "The next day he Facebook messaged me to ask if I was on birth control because the condom came off during. So off I went to the pharmacy to buy my first Plan B [morning-after pill] and fall down a mental spiral until I got my period. I never heard from that guy again and actually don't even remember his name."[65] LaRue says that she believes she would have made much better choices about sex if her parents had been more open with her.

Further investigation of sex-related conversations between parents and children also reveal that in many cases the situation is more complicated than simply telling parents to talk to their children about sex more often. Researchers have also found that even when parents do try to educate their children about sex, they often do a poor job. For example, in 2012 Planned Parenthood commissioned a survey of more than two thousand parents and teens and found significant differences in how the two groups interpret the communication about sex that happens in their families. For instance, researchers found that 42 percent of parents say they have talked to their teens about how to say no to sex, but only 27 percent of teens say they have had this conversation with their parents. Elliott explains that sex is a difficult topic to discuss. As a result, even when parents want to speak openly with their children about sex, they sometimes struggle to do so. As a result, she concludes that "parents may not be their children's best sex educators and certainly should not be their *only* sex educators."[66] Due to the miscommunication or lack of communication about sex that happens in many families, critics argue that while society should continue to encourage parents to take a more active role in their children's sex education, it should also provide youth with sex education in other ways, such as at school.

More Focus on Positives

Another critique of sex education in the United States is that most parents and educators focus on the negative consequences of sex without discussing the fact that sex can (and should) be a healthy part of human sexuality. The World Health Organization states that "sexual health is fundamental to the physical and emotional health and well-being of individuals, couples and families."[67] Although this does not mean that teens need to have sex to have good relationships, it means that they do need to learn about how sex can be a beneficial part of a relationship when they are ready for it.

Al Vernacchio is a high school sex educator who also offers workshops and lectures throughout the United States. He believes the only way for teens to grow up and have their own healthy sexual relationships is for someone to teach them how to do so. He argues that few teachers do this; instead, much teen sex education focuses on the dangers of sex. This leaves teens without an understanding of how sex can also be a part of a fulfilling relationship. He asks, "How *can* you have a good sexual relationship when no one ever tells you how to do that? There's plenty of talk about what *not* to do, but that doesn't automatically provide a road map for creating a happy and successful sexual life." Vernacchio insists that parents and teachers need to help teens learn that sex can be a healthy and fulfilling part of a relationship, not just something that can make them pregnant or give them HIV. "I can't imagine standing up in front of a class . . . and telling them that sex is going to ruin their lives," he says. "How does that help them develop a healthy sexuality? What kind of message would I be sending about intimacy, love, and relationships?"[68]

A Lack of Knowledge

Although many teens receive sex education in school, and most parents say they have talked to their children about sex, many US teens still seem ignorant about sex and sexuality. Sex advice columnist Dan Savage says he commonly gets letters from readers that reveal that teens still have huge misconceptions about sex and contraception. Some of these letters show that some teens still believe that a girl cannot get pregnant the first time she has sex or that taking a hot shower or drinking a cap full of bleach after sex will prevent pregnancy. Such ignorance frustrates him. "It's enough to make you want to put your head down on the desk and cry,"[69] he says.

> "[Teenage ignorance about sex is] enough to make you want to put your head down on the desk and cry."[69]
>
> —Sex advice columnist Dan Savage.

Actress Jane Fonda has worked with teens for years and is founder of the Georgia Campaign for Adolescent Power & Potential and the Jane Fonda Center for Adolescent Reproductive Health at Emory University School of Medicine in Georgia. She

Many experts believe the high rate of teen pregnancy in the United States is due to a lack of knowledge among teens about contraception methods, including condoms (pictured). The Centers for Disease Control and Prevention reported in 2012 that about half of teens who gave birth were not using any form of birth control.

also finds a lack of basic sexual knowledge among teens. She says that she keeps meeting teens from a wide variety of socioeconomic backgrounds who simply do not understand how their bodies work or know basic facts about pregnancy and STDs. Fonda says, "There is so much misinformation about these things floating around that I felt that the health of many teens I met—their future happiness, even—was on the line."[70]

For this reason, she wrote a book to provide teens with that understanding and information.

That lack of knowledge is having serious consequences. Many teens in the United States are engaging in sexual behavior without understanding the potential consequences and without knowing that they can protect themselves from these consequences. For example, there is evidence that the high rate of teen pregnancy in the United States is largely due to the fact that many teens do not know the importance of contraception. In a 2012 report about teen pregnancy, the CDC reported that among teens that gave birth, almost half were not using any type of birth control, and nearly a third of those did not even believe they could get pregnant. A 2014 US survey of twelve- to seventeen-year-olds by the M.A.C. AIDS Fund—an HIV/AIDS prevention and assistance program—showed that many teens also lack knowledge about HIV, a life-threatening STD. The organization found that almost nine in ten teens do not believe they are at risk for getting HIV. One-third did not even realize that HIV is an STD. Statistics such as this show that the United States needs to continue to undertake efforts to educate teens about sex and help them make good choices about sexual behavior.

> **"There is so much misinformation about these things floating around that I felt that the health of many teens I met—their future happiness, even—was on the line."[70]**
>
> *—Actress and humanitarian Jane Fonda.*

Source Notes

Introduction: A Life-Changing Choice

1. Garrison, "'Sex Is a Symbol of Popularity at My School,'" *HuffPost Teen* (blog), *Huffington Post*, October 13, 2013. www.huffingtonpost.com.
2. Elizabeth, "'I Argue with Myself Every Day About Losing My Virginity,'" *HuffPost Teen* (blog), *Huffington Post*, October 25, 2013. www.huffingtonpost.com.
3. Quoted in Avert, "First Time Sex Stories: Laura 2." www .avert.org.
4. Quoted in Avert, "First Time Sex Stories: Erin: A Meaningful Experience." www.avert.org.
5. Stephanie Faye, "I've Only Had Sex with One Person (and That's Ok)," Thought Catalog, November 1, 2013. http:// thoughtcatalog.com.
6. Bronwen Pardes, *Doing It Right: Making Smart, Safe, and Satisfying Choices About Sex*. New York: Simon Pulse, 2013, p. xii.

Chapter One: About Teen Sex Today

7. Rima Himelstein, "Why Should Teens Consider Long-Acting Reversible Contraceptive (LARC) Methods?," Philly.com, May 20, 2014. www.philly.com.
8. Quoted in American College of Obstetricians and Gynecologists, "IUDs Implants Are Most Effective Reversible Contraceptives Available," American College of Obstetricians and Gynecologists, June 20, 2011. www.acog.org.
9. Johnny, comment to K.J. Dell'Antonia, "Are Teenagers Really Having Less Sex?," *Motherlode* (blog), *New York Times*, November 16, 2011. http://parenting.blogs.nytimes.com.
10. Quoted in Kori Ellis, "Teen Talk: Does Oral Sex Count?," She Knows, May 20, 2012. www.sheknows.com.

11. Joel Best and Kathleen A. Bogle, *Kids Gone Wild: From Rainbow Parties to Sexting, Understanding the Hype over Teen Sex*. New York: New York University Press, 2014, p. 129.

12. Justin R. Garcia et al., "Sexual Hookup Culture: A Review," *Review of General Psychology*, vol. 12, no. 2, 2012. www.apa.org.

13. Lindsay Nance, "Let's Talk About Sex: Hookup Culture," *Voice of Troy*, November 24, 2014. http://thevoice.srcs.org.

14. Donna Freitas, *The End of Sex: How Hookup Culture Is Leaving a Generation Unhappy, Sexually Unfulfilled, and Confused About Intimacy*. New York: Basic, 2013, pp. 11–12.

15. Quoted in Nancy Jo Sales, "Friends Without Benefits," *Vanity Fair*, September 26, 2013. www.vanityfair.com.

16. Sales, "Friends Without Benefits."

17. Quoted in Tracy Clark-Flory, "Adolescents Aren't Having Much Sex, Despite All the Hype to the Contrary," Alternet, April 2, 2013. www.alternet.org.

Chapter Two: Influences on Teenage Sexual Behavior

18. John, "I Feel Like I'm Not a 'Man' Because I Haven't Had Sex," *HuffPost Teen* (blog), *Huffington Post*, February 3, 2015. www.huffingtonpost.com.

19. Quoted in Avert, "First Time Sex Stories: Meg." www.avert.org.

20. Quoted in TeenBreaks.com, "The Pressure for Sex." www.teenbreaks.com.

21. Quoted in Susan Scutti, "Peer Pressure, Sex, and Your Teen: Kids Are More Likely to Have Sex When They Think Everyone Else Is Doing It," Medical Daily, September 12, 2014. www.medicaldaily.com.

22. Quoted in Sales, "Friends Without Benefits."

23. Quoted in McAfee, "Teens Feeling Pressure to 'Grow Up' and Reveal Intimate Details Due to Social Networking According to McAfee Study," 2012. www.mcafee.com.

24. American College of Pediatricians, "The Teenage Brain: Under Construction," May 2011. www.acpeds.org.
25. stararoura, "Can't Stop Thinking About Sex," question to Sexual Health—Teens Message Board, HealthBoards, October 21, 2012. www.healthboards.com.
26. Planned Parenthood, "Sex, Alcohol, and Drugs." www.plannedparenthood.org.
27. Nance, "Let's Talk About Sex."
28. National Campaign to Prevent Teen and Unplanned Pregnancy, "Counting It Up: What Policymakers Can Do," May 2014. https://thenationalcampaign.org.
29. Planned Parenthood, "Half of Teens Feel Uncomfortable Talking to Their Parents About Sex While Only 19 Percent of Parents Feel the Same, New Survey Shows," October 2, 2012. www.plannedparenthood.org.
30. Best and Bogle, *Kids Gone Wild*, p. 144.
31. Carolyn C. Ross, "Overexposed and Under-prepared: The Effects of Early Exposure to Sexual Content," *Psychology Today*, August 13, 2012. www.psychologytoday.com.
32. Quoted in Wiley, "Viewing Sexually Explicit Material Is Less Associated with Young People's Sexual Behavior than Previously Thought," press release, April 25, 2013. www.wiley.com.
33. Quoted in Annie Lowrey, "MTV's '16 and Pregnant,' Derided by Some, May Resonate as a Cautionary Tale," *New York Times*, January 13, 2014. www.nytimes.com.
34. Quoted in Indiana University–Bloomington, "Study: Heavy Viewers of 'Teen Mom' and '16 and Pregnant' Have Unrealistic Views of Teen Pregnancy," January 9, 2014. http://news.indiana.edu.
35. Quoted Indiana University–Bloomington, "Study."
36. Quoted in Diane E. Levin and Jean Kilbourne, *So Sexy So Soon: The New Sexualized Childhood and What Parents Can Do to Protect Their Kids*. New York: Ballantine, 2008, p. 27.
37. Quoted in David Segal, "Does Porn Hurt Children?," *New York Times*, March 28, 2014. www.nytimes.com.

Chapter Three: The Consequences of Sexual Activity by Teens

38. Maggie, "I Had a Baby at 14, and Here's What I Now Know About Sex," *HuffPost Teen* (blog), *Huffington Post,* November 20, 2014. www.huffingtonpost.com.

39. Matt Posner and Jess C. Scott, *Teen Guide to Sex & Relationships*. JessINK, 2012, p. 23.

40. Kate, comment on StayTeen.org, "Stay Out Loud: Do You Think Teens Regret Not Waiting Longer to Have Sex?," February 20, 2014. http://stayteen.org.

41. Brooke, "Confessions of a Teenage Christian Virgin," *HuffPost Teen* (blog), Huffington Post, January 27, 2015. www.huffingtonpost.com.

42. Quoted in Rachel Simmons, "Reputation Rehab: How to Bounce Back from Rumors," *Teen Vogue,* August 2011. www.teenvogue.com.

43. Quoted in Simmons, "Reputation Rehab."

44. Quoted in Lifetime, "*The Pregnancy Project:* Book Excerpt." www.mylifetime.com.

45. Amber, "My Name Is Amber," Naked Truth, 2012. www.nakedtruth.idaho.gov.

46. Office of Adolescent Health, US Department of Health and Human Services, "Sexually Transmitted Diseases," February 27, 2015. www.hhs.gov.

47. Centers for Disease Control and Prevention, "Syphilis—CDC Fact Sheet," January 29, 2014. www.cdc.gov.

48. Life with Herpes, comment on Elizabeth Boskey, "Readers Respond: Living with Herpes," About.com, November 26, 2011. http://std.about.com.

49. Mike, "Atripla, Vivid Dreams, and Getting Past the Undetectable Brick Wall," Body, March 26, 2014. www.thebody.com.

50. Lauren Dolgen, "Why I Created MTV's '16 and Pregnant,'" CNN, May 5, 2011. www.cnn.com.

51. Quoted in Kari Huus, "A Baby Changes Everything: The True Cost of Teen Pregnancy's Uptick," NBC News, February 19, 2010. www.nbcnews.com.

52. National Campaign to Prevent Teen and Unplanned Pregnancy, "Why It Matters: Teen Childbearing, Education, and Economic Wellbeing," July 2012. https://thenationalcampaign.org.

53. S.J. Ventura, B.E. Hamilton, and T.J. Mathews, "National and State Patterns of Teen Births in the United States, 1940–2013," *National Vital Statistics Reports*, vol. 63, no. 4, 2014. www.cdc.gov.

54. Comment on Quora, "I'm 15, Only a Few of My Friends Are Virgins, and They Make Fun of Me for Only Having Pop Kissed a Guy in My Life. What Should I Do?," January 26, 2014. www.quora.com.

Chapter Four: Social Efforts to Change Teen Sexual Activity

55. Sexuality Information and Education Council of the United States, "Fact Sheet: The Division of Adolescent and School Health: Promoting Effective Sexual Health Education Programs in Schools," March 2014. http://siecus.org.

56. Beth Leyba, "Abstinence-Only Education Doesn't Work—I Know from Personal Experience," *HuffPost Politics* (blog), Huffington Post, March 4, 2014. www.huffingtonpost.com.

57. Jessica Bol, "Individual and Situational Variables: Predictors of Adolescent Risky Sexual Behavior," dissertation, California School of Professional Psychology, San Francisco Campus, Alliant International University, January 2014, p. 72.

58. Quoted in Jenelle Marie, "How Abstinence-Only Sex Ed Is Driving Up STD Rates," Take Part, April 3, 2013. www.takepart.com.

59. Quoted in Katherine Brown, "HIV Positive Student Advocates Comprehensive Sex Education," Wuft News, March 17, 2015. www.wuft.org.

60. US House of Representatives, Committee on Energy and Commerce, *A Better Approach to Teenage Pregnancy Prevention: Sexual Risk Avoidance,* July 2012. http://energycommerce.house.gov.

61. National Abstinence Education Association, "Frequently Asked Questions—Correcting Misinformation in the Sex Ed Debate." www.abstinenceassociation.org.

62. Quoted in Brigham Young University, "Good Things Come to Couples Who Wait," news release, December 22, 2010. http://news.byu.edu.

63. Samantha Pugsley, "It Happened to Me: I Waited Until My Wedding Night to Lose My Virginity and I Wish I Hadn't," XOJane, August 1, 2014. www.xojane.com.

64. Sinikka Elliott, *Not My Kid: What Parents Believe About the Sex Lives of Their Teenagers*. New York: New York University Press, 2012, p. 3.

65. Gabby LaRue, "I Plan on Being Brutally Honest About My Sex Life with My (Hypothetical) Kids," XOJane, September 23, 2014. www.xojane.com.

66. Elliott, *Not My Kid,* p. 152.

67. World Health Organization, "Developing Sexual Health Programmes: A Framework for Action," 2010. http://whqlib doc.who.int.

68. Al Vernacchio, *For Goodness Sex: Changing the Way We Talk to Teens About Sexuality, Values, and Health*. New York: HarperCollins, 2014, pp. xi, xii.

69. Quoted in *Los Angeles Times*, "The Latest from the National Desk," January 20, 2012. http://latimesblogs.latimes.com /nationnow/2012/01/nearly-1-in-3-pregnant-teens-had -no-clue-they-could-get-pregnant.html.

70. Jane Fonda, *Being a Teen: Everything Teen Girls & Boys Should Know About Relationships, Sex, Love, Health, Identity & More*. New York: Random House, 2014, p. viii.

Advocates for Youth
2000 M St. NW, Suite 750
Washington, DC 20036
phone: (202) 419-3420
fax: (202) 419-1448
website: www.advocatesforyouth.org

Advocates for Youth aims to help young people make informed, responsible decisions about their sexual health. It believes that sex education in the United States should be more positive and realistic. The group's website contains information about topics including abstinence, contraception, sexual violence, and issues specific to lesbian, gay, bisexual, and transgender youth.

Guttmacher Institute
125 Maiden Ln., 7th floor
New York, NY 10038
phone: (212) 248-1111
fax: (212) 248-1951
website: www.guttmacher.org

The Guttmacher Institute works to advance sexual and reproductive health through research, policy analysis, and public education. It publishes the journals *Perspectives on Sexual and Reproductive Health* and *International Perspectives on Sexual and Reproductive Health*, and its website includes numerous reports on teenage sexual behavior.

National Abstinence Education Association (NAEA)
1701 Pennsylvania Ave. NW, Suite 300
Washington, DC 20006
phone: (202) 248-5420
fax: (866) 935-4850

e-mail: info@thenaea.org
website: www.abstinenceassociation.org

The NAEA is an organization that works to promote abstinence-only education by educating the public and advocating for federal funding. Its website has information about the benefits of abstinence.

National Campaign to Prevent Teen and Unplanned Pregnancy

1776 Massachusetts Ave. NW, Suite 200
Washington, DC 20036
phone: (202) 478-8500
fax: (202) 478-8588
website: https://thenationalcampaign.org

The National Campaign to Prevent Teen and Unplanned Pregnancy believes that teen pregnancy is harmful to both children and parents and works to reduce the rate of teen pregnancy. Its website has numerous reports about the problems associated with teen pregnancy.

Planned Parenthood Federation of America

434 W. 33rd St.
New York, NY 10001
phone: (212) 541-7800
fax: (212) 245-1845
website: www.plannedparenthood.org

Planned Parenthood works to help people receive affordable, high-quality reproductive care. It believes that teens are empowered by comprehensive sexual information. Its website provides information about numerous sex-related topics, including sex, contraception, pregnancy, abortion, and STDs.

Sexuality Information and Education Council of the United States (SIECUS)

90 John St., Suite 402
New York, NY 10038

phone: (212) 819-9770
fax: (212) 819-9776
website: www.siecus.org

SIECUS was founded in 1964 to provide education and information about sexuality and reproductive health. It believes that sex is a fundamental part of being human and that people need comprehensive information about sex. Its website contains reports and fact sheets about sex education in the United States.

For Further Research

Books

Joel Best and Kathleen A. Bogle, *Kids Gone Wild: From Rainbow Parties to Sexting, Understanding the Hype over Teen Sex*. New York: New York University Press, 2014.

Jane Fonda, *Being a Teen: Everything Teen Girls & Boys Should Know About Relationships, Sex, Love, Health, Identity & More*. New York: Random House, 2014.

Donna Freitas, *The End of Sex: How Hookup Culture Is Leaving a Generation Unhappy, Sexually Unfulfilled, and Confused About Intimacy*. New York: Basic, 2013.

Bronwen Pardes, *Doing It Right: Making Smart, Safe, and Satisfying Choices About Sex*. New York: Simon Pulse, 2013.

Internet Sources

Advocates for Youth, "Adolescent Sexual Health and Behavior in the United States: Positive Trends and Areas in Need of Improvement," February 2012. http://advocatesforyouth.org /storage/advfy/documents/adolescent-sexual-behavior-de mographics.pdf.

Guttmacher Institute, "American Teens' Sexual and Reproductive Health," May 2014. www.guttmacher.org/pubs/FB-ATSRH .pdf.

Henry J. Kaiser Family Foundation, "Sexual Health of Adolescents and Young Adults in the United States," August 2014. http://kff.org/womens-health-policy/fact-sheet/sexual-health -of-adolescents-and-young-adults-in-the-united-states.

Jessica Lahey, "What Schools Should Teach Kids About Sex," *Atlantic,* March 6, 2015. www.theatlantic.com/educa tion/archive/2015/03/what-schools-should-teach-kids-about -sex/387061.

National Campaign to Prevent Teen and Unplanned Pregnancy, "Why It Matters: Teen Childbearing, Education, and Economic Wellbeing," July 2012. https://thenationalcampaign.org/sites/default/files/resource-primary-download/childbearing-education-economicwellbeing.pdf.

Office of Adolescent Health, US Department of Health and Human Services, "Sexually Transmitted Diseases," February 27, 2015. www.hhs.gov/ash/oah/adolescent-health-topics/reproductive-health/stds.html.

US House of Representatives, Committee on Energy and Commerce, *A Better Approach to Teenage Pregnancy Prevention: Sexual Risk Avoidance*, July 2012. http://energycommerce.house.gov/sites/republicans.energycommerce.house.gov/files/analysis/20120706riskavoidance.pdf.

Index

Note: Boldface page numbers indicate illustrations.

Picture Credits

Cover: Thinkstock Images

Focal Point/Shutterstock.com: 27

Image Point Fr/Shutterstock.com: 15

Richard Lee/KRT/Newscom: 55

MTV/Photofest: 33

David M. Phillips/Science Source: 12

Martin M. Rotker/Science Source: 42

Sokolenok/Shutterstock.com: 45

Thinkstock Images: 3, 8, 19, 25, 46, 51, 62

About the Author

Andrea C. Nakaya, a native of New Zealand, holds a BA in English and an MA in communications from San Diego State University. She has written and edited more than thirty-five books on current issues. She currently lives in Encinitas, California, with her husband and their two children, Natalie and Shane.